pocket: *adjective:* small enough to be carried in the pocket
issue: *noun:* a vital or unsettled matter

Born from a frustration with the cyclical and often shallow nature of today's "rolling" news, Pocket Issue pulls together the background to some of the biggest challenges facing our world.

We have no political agenda, our only ambition is to brief you on the global issues that affect our world – climate change, terrorism, oil shortages – giving you the confidence to hold your own at the dinner table or the water cooler.

We welcome your thoughts and comments at www.**pocket***issue*.com.

GW00382599

Pocket issue
Small briefs for a big world

Pocket Issue
The Energy Crisis

Published by Pocket Issue, London
www.**pocket** *issue*.com
info@**pocket** *issue*.com

First edition 2007
Copyright © Pocket Issue, 2007

ISBN: 978-0-9554415-0-9
ISBN: 0-9554415-0-1

The contents of this publication are believed to be correct at the
time of printing. Nevertheless, the publisher can accept no
responsibility for errors or omissions, changes in the details given,
or for any expense or loss thereby caused.

Design by sanchezdesign. www.sanchezdesign.co.uk

Pocket
ISSUE

Publishing has been no mean feat and thank you to all who have helped along the way.

In particular: Clive Weston – who very sadly did not live to see publication – who gave his interest, intelligence and support, Nat Price, Daniel Sanchez, Andrzej Krauze, Julia Hartley, Natasha Kirwan, Andrew Crompton, Richard Owen, Mary Alexander, Emily Harper, Victoria Dean, Nick Band and Rebecca Slack.

The Pocket Issue Team

Contents

One Minute Guide / *The issues in the blink of an eye*　　　9

Roots / *The important questions answered*

– **The Energy Crisis** / *Why is there an energy crisis?*　　13

– **Oil** / *Is the world's oil running out?*　　18

– **Natural Gas** / *Cash cow or big headache?*　　23

– **Coal** / *The world's dirtiest fuel?*　　27

– **Nuclear Energy** / *Low carbon saviour?*　　30

– **Renewable Energies** / *Wind, solar, biofuel…?*　　38

– **Hydrogen** / *Sky's the limit or pie in the sky?*　　46

The Key Players / *The people and institutions that will influence our lives in the UK*　　49

Stargazing / *What would be a good and bad scenario come 2030?*　　57

What can you do? / *How you can make a mark*　　63

Further Reading / *The best places to keep up-to-date*　　69

The Glossary / *Jargon-free explanations*　　73

One Minute Guide

The issues in the blink of an eye

ONE MINUTE GUIDE

Addicted to oil
Over 85% of the world's energy – the heat, the light, the power,
the fuel – come from fossil fuels: oil, gas and coal.

Global warming
The gases emitted from burning fossil fuels are the major
contributor to climate change. We need another way to power
our planet to avoid changing it forever.

Finite fuels
Oil and gas are running out. Pessimistic forecasters see them
trailing off from 2008, bolder analysts closer to 2040.
We have more breathing space with coal.

Running dry
Over the past 20 years world demand for energy has doubled.
In the next 20 it is set to rise by 50%. The "new" economies, led
by China and India, are driving this surge.

Security
Energy is a political issue. Importers of fossil fuels, such as the
UK, will increasingly rely on suppliers with whom we have
uneasy relations – for example Iran and Russia.

Mind the gap
Many countries are unsure how to power their futures. In the UK,
ageing coal and nuclear power stations will close over the next
decade leaving an "energy gap" that needs to be filled.

What next?
Economies need reliable and cheap power to help them grow.
What will supply this? Coal, nuclear or renewable energy?

Clean coal?
New ways to clean up coal – the most plentiful but the dirtiest of
the fossil fuels – are under investigation. Chief amongst them is
capturing carbon dioxide and holding it underground

Going nuclear?
Nuclear is reliable in output and low carbon. It is also safer than
it has ever been. That's why the UK is planning to build a new
generation of nuclear power stations. But the cost, the harmful
waste and the impact on the energy market are problems.

Green shoots?
A tiny amount of the world's energy comes from renewable
sources – e.g. the sun, the wind, the sea or plant life – but more
will be needed in the battle against global warming.

H2 Oh?
Hydrogen is the most common element potentially available
to man. It can be used to fuel power stations and it's clean
and efficient. But getting hold of it cheaply is a problem, so
is storage.

The world's problem
Energy – how we get it, what we do with it, who we rely on –
is a problem not just for governments but for all of us.
Decisions made now will change our world for ever.

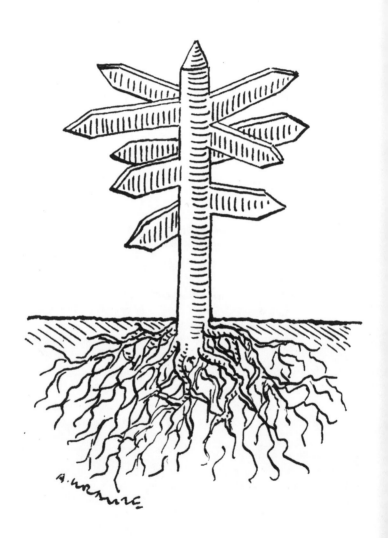

Roots

*The important
questions answered*

THE ENERGY CRISIS

Open a newspaper in the past year and you will have read of record gas and petrol prices in the UK; oil companies reporting record profits; oil being the motivation for the Iraq war; the UK opposing Iran's nuclear ambitions whilst planning to reinvest in its own nuclear programme. Lurking behind this tangle of stories is "energy".

Why is there an energy crisis?
The fuels that have powered our lives for the last century – oil, gas and coal – are running out. At the same time, energy demand is set to increase by 60% by 2030, both from the developed world and the hungry, "new" economies such as China and India.

Alternatives – for example nuclear power or renewable energy sources such as wind and solar power are either controversial or unproven, or both.

> The world's energy demand is set to increase by 60% by 2030

What about global warming?
Carbon released when fossil fuels are burned is now thought to be the biggest contributor to global warming. Even with an infinite supply of these fuels, we would need to find other ways to power our planet.

The Villains - the leading carbon emitters

Rest of World 40%
USA 24%
UK 2%
Russia 6%
EU 12%
China 16%

Source: DTI

What do we mean by "energy"?
Two things. It is what we need to propel us around the world by car and plane (usually oil burned in engines) and, secondly, the electricity (or natural gas) required to heat and power homes, factories and offices.

Is electricity a fuel, like oil or coal?

No. It's a convenient way to transfer energy. It is generated from primary energy sources, such as coal or natural gas.

Most electricity in the world is produced in power stations. Copper wires collect an electrical charge from magnets spun by turbines. These turbines are usually driven by steam from water heated by burning coal, gas, or by heat from nuclear fission. However, turbines can also be turned by water flowing through hydro-electric dams or tidal generators, or by the wind.

Can electricity be stockpiled, like gas or coal?

No. Electricity differs from other forms of energy as there is no economic way to store significant amounts of it. Therefore supply has to meet demand neatly. This is important when considering renewable energies that rely on nature and whose output is uneven.

Who uses the most energy in the world?

The USA, but countries such as China, Russia and India, with growing populations and economies, are catching up fast. Over the last decade, China's energy consumption has grown seven times faster than the USA's. The chart below shows another angle, the amount of energy used per head of population.

Energy consumption per person
Units: Million Btu

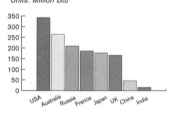

Source: EIA

Why have we become reliant on fossil fuels?

They have a high energy content, have been historically inexpensive, and are relatively easy to store and transport.

> Over the last decade, China's energy consumption has grown seven times as fast as the USA's

hold the greatest stocks – gas in Russia or oil in Iran and Saudi Arabia – have historically had uneasy relationships with the West. The fear is that instability in these countries will affect the price of fuels or that supplies could be withheld in times of political crisis.

And where are the fossil fuels?

Spread around the world, but the most significant future sources of oil and natural gas are located in the Middle East and Russia. Which raises the issue of "energy security".

Energy security?

It's how much control a nation has over its energy supplies.

"Western" economies rely on fossil fuels to feed their growth. For many years these countries were self-sufficient but most now depend on imports. With the arrival of the new economies, more hands are fighting for their share of a shrinking cake.

Things are further complicated because the countries who

Doesn't the UK have a lot of oil and gas rigs in the North Sea? Aren't we energy secure?

Not any more. Since the 1960's we have been "rich" in oil and especially in natural gas, exporting it to other countries. However, over the last forty years our reserves have been exploited so that since 2005 we have needed other countries to help supply us.

Where do we source our energy?
Units: kWh

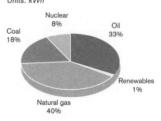

Nuclear 8%
Coal 18%
Oil 33%
Renewables 1%
Natural gas 40%

Source: DTI

What is LPG?

Liquefied Petroleum Gas, commonly known as "Auto-gas". It is a natural by-product of the drilling process and can also be refined from crude oil. It emits less carbon in comparison to petrol or diesel and is increasingly available in the UK as a fuel for cars and an alternative to natural gas in homes and industry.

OIL IN THE WORLD TODAY

How does the world use its oil?

Over 90% is used to fuel transport, a little is used in power stations and generators, and the rest in the manufacture of pharmaceuticals and plastics.

Who are the world's biggest oil consumers?
Units: Thousand barrels daily

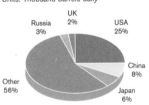

USA 25%
China 8%
Japan 6%
Other 56%
Russia 3%
UK 2%

Source: IEA 2006

Over 90% of the world's oil is used to fuel transport

And who has the most oil?

Saudi Arabia, Iran and Iraq have the greatest proven stocks (about 40% of the world's total).

Does the UK have any oil?

Yes. We produce 2% of the world's oil, though our stocks are running out.

What about the oil sands?

Over 75% are thought to be in Canada and Venezuela. If they are included in the oil inventory, Canada would be second only to Saudi Arabia in reserves.

Who controls oil production?

The big oil companies such as BP, Exxon Mobil and Shell play an important role in bringing oil to the market in the Western world.

However, over 75% of the world's remaining oil is in the hands of government-owned oil

19

companies, the biggest being those in Saudi Arabia and Iran.

OPEC, the Organisation of Petroleum Exporting Countries, is an alliance of 11 of these nationalised oil companies in the Middle East, Africa, South America and Asia (see The Key Players). OPEC countries are responsible for 40% of current production and have two-thirds of future reserves.

How do oil companies make such big profits?
The big oil companies make money out of finding and drilling for oil rather than the refining and selling, especially when oil prices are very high.

What influences the oil price?
Supply and demand. World demand is set to increase by 40% by 2030. Supply is more fickle. Big weather events, such as Hurricane Katrina, can disrupt it, as can political instability, such as the war in Iraq. OPEC countries also try to ration the amount of oil they release to the market to maintain a good price.

Are oil companies responsible for high petrol prices?
Not really. It is the government - through tax - that takes most of the money. Garages make more money on a pint of milk than on a litre of petrol.

Who takes the money at the petrol pump?
Units: Based on 90p litre of petrol

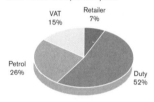

Source: Petrolprices.com

OIL / THE FUTURE

How much oil is there left?
It's guesswork. Some
estimates place 30 to 40
years of oil reserves based
on current production.

What are "reserves"?
The amount of oil in the
ground that is economically
viable to recover. Estimates
look at proven, probable and
possible reserves.

Why is it guesswork?
Partly because it is not an
exact science, and also
because certain countries -
including some members of
OPEC - do not allow
independent audits.

*Do we know when oil is going
to start running out?*
Not for sure, it's a matter of
heated scientific debate, called
"Peak Theory." This is the date
that world oil production peaks
and subsequently begins its
decline - the date we start
running out of oil.

What is the timeline?
Gloomy forecasters see world

production peaking in 2008,
more optimistic analysts
estimate closer to 2040.

*What's so important about
this peak, won't there still
be oil?*
Yes, but it will become more
expensive as demand outstrips
supply. Also, if there are no
viable "replacement" energy
sources, there is likely to be a
knock-on effect on the price of
other fossil fuels, such as
natural gas and coal.

Prices will go up, is that it?
Possibly. However, rising oil
prices could also have political
consequences, affecting
political stability by pushing up
inflation and forcing
governments onto the back
foot. For example, in the 1973
Arab-Israeli War OPEC
stopped exporting oil to
countries that backed Israel,
including the USA and UK, the
catalyst to a global recession
the following year.

Oil plays a significant role in
international relations.
Suspicion surrounds the US's
motivation in invading Iraq.

21

Iran's current foreign policy is thought to be indirectly encouraged by support from China, who want direct access to Iranian oil.

How has the price of oil changed?
Units: US Dollars

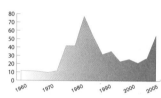

Source: BP

Is there a chance that new oil reserves will be found?
Possible, but unlikely. Experts don't expect to find significant new reserves though the search continues. Possible areas include Russia, Alaska and West Africa. Synthetic oils – for example from oil sands – are likely to make some contribution in the future.

OIL / THE ISSUES

Oil provides the world with 40% of its energy.

90% of the world's oil is used in transport.

The USA uses over a quarter of the world's oil.

The greatest stocks are found in Saudi Arabia and Iran. Canada has the greatest oil sands reserves.

The world's oil is running out. Estimates range from 2008 to 2037 as the date production "peaks".

NATURAL GAS

Nearly 25% of the world's energy comes from natural gas. Over the past 40 years, it has been the most important fuel in the UK, yet prices are rising and the UK's reserves are running out.

THE BACKGROUND

What is natural gas?
Mainly methane and created, like oil, through the work of heat and pressure on decaying plants and animals. Natural gas is often found where oil is found.

Where do we get it from?
Like oil, we drill for it. It can also be a natural by-product of drilling for oil. There are natural gas-only fields that tend to be located deeper in the earth's crust.

Does natural gas need to be refined like oil?
No. The big challenge is its distribution. Pipelines - often crossing continents - are one answer, and also LNG.

23

LNG?

Liquefied natural gas. It is natural gas condensed and transported as a liquid. LNG is expensive and extremely volatile. Its major importance in the future could be in adding diversity to the market, so we are less reliant on a limited number of suppliers and pipelines.

NATURAL GAS IN THE WORLD TODAY

How does the world use its natural gas?

Primarily in heating homes and businesses, and also in generating electricity. Some is used in agriculture.

Who has the world's natural gas reserves?
Units: % of the worlds total (trillion cubic meter)

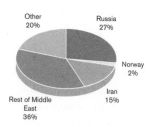

Source: IEA

Who are the world's biggest consumers?

The USA and Russia. The UK is third.

Why is natural gas an important fuel in the UK?

Because of our gas fields in the North Sea. It provides 37% of our electricity and a substantial part of our heating needs.

Does the UK make its electricity?
Units: kWh

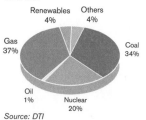

Source: DTI

Why have gas prices risen so high in recent years?

We have had relatively cheap gas for a number of years but with North Sea fields in decline and a reliance on overseas partners, prices were always likely to rise. High prices in the 2005/6 winter came from some European neighbours stockpiling reserves rather than passing on supply to the UK market. There was also a fire in

24

one of the major storage facilities in the North Sea. Storage is one of the UK's main challenges. Compared to other European countries we have not invested in enough spare capacity for the "rainy days".

NATURAL GAS / THE FUTURE

Is the world's natural gas running out in the same way as oil?
Yes. Cautious estimates suggest a peak by 2020, with maybe around 70 years of reserves based on current production.

How much do we have left in the UK?
We have gone from riches to rags in less than fifty years, and by 2020 we will be importing 90% of our natural gas.

So natural gas isn't a "secure" energy source for the UK?
As we are now importers, no. However, much of the slack in the short to medium term will be taken up by Norway, who,

> By 2020 the UK will be importing 90% of its natural gas

disregarding the odd flare up over cod, should be a reliable supplier. Russia, Nigeria, Algeria and Iran - all less "Norwegian" in political outlook – will also have a role.

How does the UK receive its imported gas?
Two main pipelines. The "Interconnector" that links us, through Belgium, to the European grid, and the new Langeled pipe from Norway. The UK has no LNG capacity at the moment, but three new terminals are being built.

Will new reserves of natural gas be found?
There are untapped reserves of methane beneath the permafrost of Siberia. There are also sources of gas mixed with frozen water, called gas hydrates, trapped on the ocean floor. It is currently not

economic to drill for them.
Though not a happy thought,
they could be unlocked by
global warming.

NATURAL GAS / THE ISSUES

Natural gas provides the world with 23% of its energy.

It has been the most important fuel in the UK over
recent decades.

By 2020, the UK will be importing 90% of its natural
gas needs. Much of this will be from Norway.

The biggest reserves are found in Russia and Iran.

The world's natural gas is running out. Cautious estimates
see a peak in 2020.

COAL

27% of the world's energy comes from coal. It is the largest fuel source for global electricity production. What's more, reserves of coal are more extensive than of oil or gas.

THE BACKGROUND

What is coal?

Coal, like natural gas and oil, is the product of heat and pressure working on plant life over time. Coal seams are formed from vegetation that accumulated in peat bogs and swamps.

How do we get hold of coal?

Coal is mined, either underground or surface (open-pit) mining. Its quality varies, depending on the percentage of carbon and moisture it contains (high carbon, low moisture makes the best coal).

COAL IN THE WORLD TODAY

How does the world use its coal?

The two major uses are in generating electricty and in the production of steel.

What are world coal reserves like?

Larger than those of oil and natural gas. Based on current consumption, estimates say that coal could last up to 150 years, though this does not take into account increased demand as other fossil fuels reserves deplete.

Where are the world's coal reserves?
Units: Million tonnes

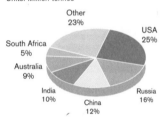

Source: IEA

And who uses the most ?

China and the USA.

How important is coal in the UK?

The UK is the 15th biggest consumer in the world. Nearly 40% of our electricity comes from 14 coal-fired power

27

stations, though some of these are coming to the end of their working lives. This rose to 50% in the winter of 2005/6 due to the high natural gas prices.

Didn't the UK close all its coal mines in the 1980's?
There are still around 40 working coal mines in the UK, though there were 200 a decade ago. Coal from the UK provides about 7% of the nation's energy. Its long term future is uncertain, with doubts over its economic viability and the high levels of sulphur most contains.

Where does the UK get its coal from?
A number of sources; big suppliers are South Africa, Australia, Russia, Colombia and Indonesia.

COAL / THE FUTURE

If there is so much coal around, why don't we use more?
Fears over global warming. Coal releases nearly three times more carbon than natural gas when burned in a power

station. However, there are attempts to make coal cleaner.

Clean coal?
The big hope is carbon capture and storage (CCS, sometimes called carbon sequestration). Carbon released when coal is burned is captured and stored. In the UK's case this could be in the empty oil and gas reservoirs beneath the North Sea. The Norwegian oil company, Statoil, is already doing this, though worries remain over the cost and the uncertain environmental impact.

Is carbon capture and storage the only technology?
No. The USA are keen on gasification, turning the coal into a gas (mainly carbon monoxide and hydrogen) that can be used in place of natural gas. The excess carbon is captured. Less substantial technologies are already in action. Coal can be "washed" prior to burning to remove impurities and improve efficiency. It can also be "co-fired" in power stations, replacing an amount of the coal with biomass (plant or animal

by-products). This technique still produces more carbon than a natural gas fired station.

40% of the UK's electricity comes from coal-fired power stations

Given coal reserves, could it be a long-term solution in the UK?

Yes, but due to carbon emissions only if CCS is viable. However, the aim of the UK government is to reduce its carbon emissions. And if you want carbon-free power, you need to look beyond fossil fuels, towards alternatives such nuclear power, renewable energies or maybe even hydrogen.

COAL / THE ISSUES

Coal provides the world with 27% of its energy.

In the UK, 40% of our electricity comes from coal.

There are more coal reserves than of oil or natural gas. The biggest are in the USA and China.

Coal releases more carbon when burned than oil or gas.

Clean coal technologies may make it an important fuel for the future.

NUCLEAR

About 6% of the world's energy comes from nuclear power.
It is deemed a low carbon technology and reliable. On the other
hand it has the reputation of being expensive, the potential to
cause catastrophic damage if things go "wrong" and creates
a waste product that is highly dangerous.

THE BACKGROUND

*How is nuclear
power generated?*
Through nuclear fission.
A chain reaction is started by
splitting an atom - usually
uranium - which releases
energy and small particles
called neutrons. These
neutrons go on to split more
atoms, each time releasing
energy and more neutrons.
The chain reaction is controlled
and produces heat used to
create steam that drives the
turbines of the power station.

What is uranium and how do we get hold of it?

Uranium is a natural element that can be mined where large reserves exist. The biggest reserves are found in Australia, Kazakhstan and Canada. After mining, the uranium needs be "enriched" for use in a power station.

What is enriched uranium and why does it need to be enriched?

It's back to the chemistry lab. Atoms of uranium have different weights based on the number of neutrons in the atom. These atoms are called isotopes. Most nuclear power stations use one such isotope, Uranium-235 (235 being the total number of protons and neutrons in the atom), that is especially prone to fission.

U-235 is found in less than 1% of the world's uranium. For an effective chain reaction to take place, uranium ore needs to be concentrated ("enriched") so it holds 2-3% of the U-235 isotope.

How is uranium enriched?

Either through a chemical process - such as diffusion by gas - or by spinning the uranium very fast to collect and concentrate the U-235 isotope.

Can uranium other than U-235 be used in a power station?

In principle, yes. 99% of the world's uranium is the isotope Uranium-238. There is another nuclear energy technology - called "breeder"- that can use the U-238 uranium to start the chain reaction (turning it into the fissionable Plutonium-239) and that also creates more fuel in the process (hence the name, breeder).

The technology is still economically unproven. Currently there is only one breeder reaction operating in the world, in Russia. However, China, Japan, India and Russia are all exploring this area.

Are there other new technologies?

The big hope is nuclear fusion - joining the nuclear atom, rather than splitting, it to release energy. Fusion offers many potential positives. The waste takes much less time to become harmless (maybe 50-100 years rather than thousands) and a fusion reactor could be safer as it does not rely on a initiating a chain reaction that could run out of control.

It is not yet clear if a fusion reactor could ever be economically viable. Because of the intense heat needed to "fuse" the atoms, experimental fusion reactors use more energy than they create. It's a physicist's joke that fusion has been "just decades away" for many decades.

Is uranium the only source of nuclear power?

U-235 is the most commonly used. The isotope Plutonium 239 is also used.

Other fuels under research are thorium for use in nuclear fission, and isotopes of hydrogen and lithium in nuclear fusion.

Is uranium a finite resource, like fossil fuels?

Yes. Based on current use there are about fifty years worth of proven U-235 reserves. If nuclear power was to produce 10% of the increasing world energy demand, it is estimated that 1000 new nuclear power stations would need to be built and reserves could drop below twenty years. There are hundreds of years of U-238 reserves.

Uranium reserves are within fifty years of exhaustion

How about the other nuclear fuels?

Thorium is more plentiful than uranium (indeed, India, with large thorium reserves, aims to switch to it when technology allows). The fusion fuels are plentiful.

What happens when the U-235 runs out?

Supporters of nuclear power argue that, with increased demand, either new uranium ore deposits could be found or that extraction from sources that are currently not viable - such as from granite or sea water - may become economic. Additionally new technologies may ease the burden on U-235. There is an element of "if" here, with no proven solutions existing.

NUCLEAR ENERGY IN THE WORLD TODAY

How does the world use its nuclear power?

Mainly in the production of electricity. The USA is the biggest producer whilst France draws the largest proportion of its energy (nearly 80%) from nuclear sources (Lithuania does more, but only has one power station!).

The world's biggest nuclear power consumers.
Units: Share of world's total (terawatt hours)

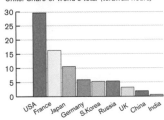

Source: BP

What about in the UK?

Nearly 20% of the UK's electricity currently comes from 14 nuclear power stations, all reaching the end of their working lives. If no new investment occurs, nuclear will provide only 4% of the UK's energy needs in 2020, leaving us with a possible energy gap. The current Labour government has stressed the need for a new generation of nuclear power stations, though this judgement has been challenged in court by Greenpeace.

> Nuclear provides about 20% of the UK's electricity. This would drop to 4% in 2020 with no reinvestment

Why do nuclear power stations need to be closed?

Age. All nuclear power stations have been designed for a specific lifespan. In some cases, these could be extended if it was deemed safe and economic to do so.

Why is the UK government so keen on nuclear power?
Global warming and energy security. Nuclear power stations release little carbon into the air and provide some self-sufficiency. Nuclear also plugs more easily into the UK's centralised power network.

Why nuclear rather than renewables, such as wind or solar?
At the moment, a few big power stations provide our homes and industry with the cheap, "always-on" electricity that we need. Renewable energies - considered intermittent and expensive - cannot currently support this centralised system. Therefore, in the short-term, nuclear seems our only alternative to fossil fuels.

Is nuclear energy "green"?
Day-to-day operation is close to being carbon neutral. Critics note that plenty of carbon is released in the mining and preparation of uranium, in the power station set-up and closing, and in handling the

waste. However, this is still much lower than the operation of, say, a natural-gas fired power station, which is the cleanest of the fossil fuels.

How many nuclear power stations does the UK government intend to build? And where?
The government sees this as a decision for the private companies who will finance the build. It is likely that many will be placed at the sites of existing nuclear facilities.

NUCLEAR ENERGY /
THE FUTURE

Why is the debate so heated over nuclear energy?
Advocates see it as the only answer to the twin demons of global warming and energy security. Critics fear the impact of its three-pronged pitchfork - radioactive waste, safety and cost.

What is the issue with waste?
There are different types of waste from the nuclear process, with different levels of radioactivity. The high-level

waste is the used fuel - usually uranium or plutonium - that remains potentially harmful for hundreds or thousands of years.

The key issue is where to store this waste safely. Storage is usually in concrete silos, though other ideas, such as disposal in the earth's crust, are deemed possible, with one such facility having been built in Finland. There is, as yet, no clear solution to this problem.

How much waste does a nuclear power station produce?

A large nuclear power station creates about 30 tonnes of waste a year. A comparable coal burning station would produce 300,000 tonnes of ash. The problem is the radioactivity.

> A large nuclear power station creates about 30 tonnes of waste a year

Can any of the waste be recycled?

Yes, reprocessing pulls out the "live" elements that can be used again as fuel - such as uranium or plutonium. Reprocessing reduces the radioactivity of the remaining waste, but is also an expensive process, currently more so than buying new uranium supplies.

The UK has a reprocessing centre in the north of Scotland. However, it has proved to be costly and has an uneven environmental record. Reprocessing is illegal in the USA due to fears that nuclear materials may get into the wrong hands.

Are nuclear power stations safe?

Most nuclear power stations run safely. Given the potential for destruction there is a natural nervousness about them. Headline disasters - for example Chernobyl in 1986 - tend to stick in the public mind. Although fatalities were relatively low, there was widespread radioactive contamination.

Chernobyl was caused by human failure. Technology moves us forward, and "passively safe" systems can now shut down power stations without need for human intervention. Safety concerns, however, don't just rest around the day-to-day running of the power stations.

Terrorism?
Nuclear power stations are an obvious target for terrorist attacks in the future. However, even critics of nuclear energy admit that this threat can be limited through design and security. There is also the threat of rogue individuals and states getting their hands on the raw materials for nuclear warheads.

Can the uranium used in nuclear power stations be used for a nuclear bomb?
Not directly. The uranium used in power stations is enriched so that about 3% is the fissionable uranium-235. A nuclear bomb, if it is to be kept to a sensible size, needs the uranium to be enriched to above 80% (Hiroshima was

90%+) though less effective "dirty bombs" could be made from material enriched to as little as 20%. However, the factories used to enrich uranium for energy use could produce weapons-grade uranium covertly. Hence the stand-off between the USA and Iran over the latter's nuclear plans.

And what about cost?
Is nuclear power more expensive than other sources, e.g. coal, gas or wind?
A like-for-like figure is hard to establish. The cost of nuclear is comparable with gas or coal, but becomes cheaper if, as seems likely, a price is placed on carbon emissions. Wind power starts cheaply, but increases if account is taken for "stand-by" capacity on calm days.

Will investment in nuclear power mean less money for new energy sources?
In principle, no. New nuclear build is to be paid for by private companies and legislation now has it that power companies draw 15% of their energy from

renewable sources (the "Renewables Obligation").

The concern is that, over time, tax-payer's money will be needed to support the nuclear industry (for example, if the government takes responsibility for closing down power stations safely) and that the focus will slip from developing new, renewable sources.

Costs of UK electricity sources
Units: Pence per KWh

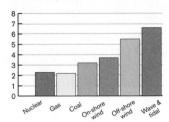

Source: Royal Society of Engineering, 2004

NUCLEAR / THE ISSUES

6% of the world's energy comes from nuclear power.

Nuclear contributes 20% of the UK's electricity needs. This will fall to 4% in fifteen years if no new investment.

The world's Uranium-235 reserves are under pressure.

Nuclear is a low carbon technology. It also provides some energy security.

Critics dislike the cost, the radioactive waste and its safety record.

New technologies – e.g. fusion – could provide long-term solutions.

RENEWABLE ENERGY

7% of the world's energy comes from renewable sources, mostly hydro-electricity. Renewable energies harness the environment around us. They are low carbon technologies and do not rely on overseas suppliers, pipelines or tankers.

The flip side is that many of the technologies are still in their infancy, and there are worries over reliability, cost and, ironically, their effect on our habitat.

THE BACKGROUND

How is renewable energy defined?
Renewable energy comes from sources that are not expected to run out within thousands or millions of years.

What gives us our renewable energy?
The heat of the sun (solar). The strength of the wind. The flow of water. The heat within the ground (geo-thermal). Hydrogen. Biomass.

Biomass?
Sometimes called bio-fuels. The by-products of animals and plants, for example car fuel refined from sugar cane, natural gas from rotting organic waste in landfill sites.

Renewable energy comes from sources not expected to run out within, say, thousands or millions of years

How do renewable energy sources create power?
In a number of different ways. Wind and water turn turbines to create electricity. Heat from solar and geo-thermal energy can raise steam for the same purpose, or be used directly for hot water and central-heating in homes, offices and factories. Photovoltaic (PV) solar panels transform the heat of the sun directly to electrical energy.

Bio-fuels or hydrogen can be used instead of oil as fuel, or potentially burned in power stations

RENEWABLE ENERGY IN TODAY'S WORLD

How much of the UK's energy comes from renewable sources?
4% in 2005. The government's aim is to increase this to 20% by 2020, part of their commitment to reduce greenhouse gases as agreed at the Kyoto meeting of 1997.

Kyoto?
A UN agreement to fight climate change. The UK, as part of the EU, has pledged to cut carbon emissions to 8% below its 1990 levels. The USA and Australia have refused to sign-up, partly because they feel it is unfair that "developing" countries, including China and India, were not bound to comply in order to give them some economic "catch-up" time.

**Who produces the most
renewable energy?**
*Units: Percentage share of world
consumption(million tonnes of oil equivalent)*

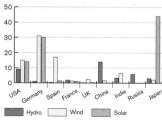

Source: BP Annual Statistical Review 2006

Why does the UK lag behind?
A lack of investment, probably
born from having secure natural
gas supplies for so long.

*How will the UK source its
renewable energy?*
Currently, the biggest source of
renewable energy in the UK is
hydro-electric power - the flow
of water through dams -
providing about 2% of our
energy. However, the best sites
have been exploited and major
growth is unlikely. The sources
with most potential are wind,
tidal and wave, and solar.

Wind power?
There are nearly 2000 wind
turbines at work in the UK
making enough energy for one
million homes. Given our

position, perched on the edge
of the Atlantic, we have the
greatest potential for wind
power in Europe, yet currently
it supplies less than 1% of our
needs - substantially lower than
Germany or Spain.
This is likely to expand. More
turbines will be built on-shore,
and more located out to sea -
off-shore - where the winds are
stronger and more reliable.

**4% of the UK's
energy currently
comes from
renewable sources**

Tidal and wave?
The potential of the strong
tides found along the UK's
coasts and estuaries, especially
in north-west Scotland and
south-west England, has been
eyed for many years. As has
the energy carried by storm
waves in both the Atlantic and
the North Sea. Compared to
wind, marine technology is still
in its infancy, with very few
schemes beyond the "pilot"
stage. Successful tidal projects
do exist in France, Canada
and Russia.

Solar?

Despite the UK's weather, solar power can work. Again, we lag behind European neighbours, such as The Netherlands or Germany, due to investment. The role of solar is more likely to be at a "micro" level, supplying electricity or heating to individual homes, offices and factories from panels positioned on buildings.

RENEWABLE ENERGY / THE FUTURE

Why is renewable energy viewed as unreliable?

Have you ever driven along a motorway and seen a row of wind turbines not spinning? Some renewable energy sources - notably wind and solar - rely on the work of mother nature. So when the wind doesn't blow or the sun doesn't shine... It is argued that wind turbines, for example, run for 75-80% of the time. However, within this "up-time", output can vary significantly, based on variables such as wind speed or air density, so that on average output is less than a third of total capacity.

> There are nearly 2000 wind turbines are at work in the UK making enough energy for one million homes

Is renewable energy less reliable than other energy sources?

Yes. No power station works at 100% capacity, due to the need for maintenance or unforeseen events. But if you compare the load factors - i.e. the percentage of "up-time" - of different energy technologies, renewable energies fall short of fossil fuel or nuclear power plants.

Why is reliability a problem, can't we just use it when it's available?

Yes, but to keep the lights on a back-up power is needed from fossil fuels or nuclear. This back-up, called "spinning reserve", is always required as no power station, however fuelled, is 100% reliable. If greater reliance is placed on

41

renewables, then more reserve might be needed.

Can renewables ever be more than an expensive "top-up"?
Possibly. Moving to tidal (which is entirely predictable) or off-shore wind power could provide a more reliable base to work from.

A greater number of renewable installations across and around the whole of the UK would also iron out local variations, though this would bring with it the charge of environmental vandalism.

Environmental vandalism?
To some. Increasing capacity would need a change in how we use and view our landscape.

This is not just NIMBYism, worrying about the view from the weekend Cornish cottage, but deeper concerns about how we alter the natural balance for our flora and fauna. How a barrage across the River Severn would affect birdlife or a rise in demand for "bio" crops might lead to

deforestation as countries switch to more intensive farming. Deforestation is thought responsible for nearly a fifth of man-made global warming.

Comparison of reliability of energy sources.
Units: Percentage "up-time"

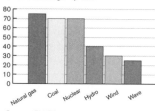

Source: BWEA

Are renewable energies more expensive than fossil fuels or nuclear sources?
Yes. Though we may need to accept that as fossil fuels dwindle energy prices will continue to rise.

What makes renewable energy expensive?
Set-up costs are high due to the new technologies involved, the construction and maintenance of the sites and the need to plug the energy into the existing system.

Are there solutions?

If investment continues, it is likely that innovation will both improve efficiency and also bring down the cost of production.

To bring renewables on-board, a change of system may be needed, moving from our heavily centralised system to one that is devolved, popularly known as micro-generation.

Micro-generation?

Bringing the supply of energy closer to the consumer. Micro-generation usually refers to small-scale generation for homes and offices.

Examples include solar panels for heating water or creating electricity, "mini" wind turbines, ground source heat pumps that use the warmth within the soil to heat in the winter and cool in the summer, burning biomass in stoves, or boilers that use excess heat to generate electricity.

"Distributed energy", larger scale energy production that goes directly to the local community rather than feeding a national grid, is also an option. This could be from wind farms, bigger solar installations, or power stations that share their waste heat with offices and factories nearby (combined heat and power or CHP stations).

In both cases it is possible to sell any excess energy back to the National Grid.

How much energy is generated like this?

Less than 1% for micro-generation. 7% of the UK's energy is supplied by CHPs, mostly in industrial use.

Why so little?

Cost. For large-scale production the main headaches are from connecting to the grid and also delays due to planning rules.

For micro-generation, costs lie with the hardware. Recouping an investment in solar panels through savings on energy bills and "sell-backs" to the grid would take 5 to 10 years.

43

Investment in a solar panel would be paid back in 5 to 10 years

Are there solutions?
Again, innovation could bring the cost of the technology down and solar panels, though expensive, are now within reach of the general public, for example sold by high street retailers, such as B&Q.

Changes in the network are a question of money and state of mind rather than technology. Energy companies will need a combination of carrot and stick to push this forward.

Who is investing in renewable energy - the government or private companies?
The mantra is that private business invests and government builds a framework that creates some certainty in the market. A Renewables Obligation states that energy companies must source 15% of their energy from renewable sources

by 2020 (this could rise to 20% if legislation is passed). Some critics say, with some reason, that the government has only created a framework for a framework - its White Paper often calls for further research or commissions rather than hard-and-fast boundaries.

As with any new technology, which horse to back is not an easy decision. However, investors are excited. Nearly 10% of US venture capital money is forecast to be invested in renewable energy schemes.

Nearly 10% of all US venture capital money is forecast to be invested in renewable energy schemes

Can renewables and nuclear be compatible?
Potentially. The fears are that a heavy investment in nuclear

44

locks us into a centralised system for the next 50 years, undermining concepts such as micro-generation and energy-saving, and drawing money away from new, renewable technologies.

A contrary viewpoint is that nuclear provides a low carbon breathing space to power the gap between the end of fossil fuels and renewables coming of age.

Do bio-fuels play a role in the UK?

A minor one in the generation of electricity and fuelling transport. You can already buy a blended bio-fuel (5% bio-fuel, the rest petrol) at many petrol stations. As we have seen, co-firing biomass with coal in power stations is already happening. Methane from landfill sites and use of organic waste for fuel are also viewed as viable, though it is unlikely they are going to make a big contribution to meeting the Government's targets.

Bio-fuels for transport, such as ethanol, are also in their infancy. Over 90% of production is focussed in two countries - the USA and Brazil - and it is less than 1% of annual world oil production.

RENEWABLE ENERGY / THE ISSUES

Renewable energy currently meets 7% of the world's needs. Most is hydro-electric power which has limited room for growth.

In the UK, 4% of our energy comes from renewables.

Renewable energy is low carbon and energy secure.

Critics bemoan the cost and its lack of reliability.

In the UK, we are aiming for 20% of our energy to come from renewables by 2020. Wind, solar and marine seem the most likely sources.

45

HYDROGEN

Hydrogen is the most plentiful element in the universe and has been mooted as an alternative "fuel" for many decades now.

THE BACKGROUND

How does hydrogen produce energy?

It releases energy when combined with oxygen, either by being burned or transferred into electrical energy in a fuel cell.

What is a fuel cell?

It's like a battery, but does not run-down or need recharging. All it requires is access to a fuel - usually hydrogen - to keep creating energy.

Why is hydrogen attractive?

Firstly, it is clean. In a hydrogen fuel cell the main waste product is water.

Secondly, it is more efficient. In car trials, hydrogen - either burned or in a fuel cell - creates at least 20% more energy than the equivalent amount of petrol or diesel. Since hydrogen is so plentiful, it also has the potential to close the door on the issue of energy security as all nations could have equal access to the fuel.

Finally, hydrogen could be an answer to problems of "storing" energy. Unlike electricity, which needs to be produced and consumed at the same rate, hydrogen could be stockpiled for future use.

HYDROGEN IN THE WORLD TODAY.

Is hydrogen being used as a fuel source today?

Not past the trial stage. Iceland has taken some steps to moving towards creating a "hydrogen economy."

The US and Russia have tested hydrogen fuelled commercial jets, while, closer to home, London Transport are experimenting with a fleet of hydrogen fuel cell buses.

HYDROGEN / THE FUTURE

What are the problems with hydrogen?

Pure hydrogen is not freely available. It cannot be drilled for or mined. Most commercial hydrogen comes as a bi-product of burning fossil fuels (with the resulting output of carbon into the air) or by a chemical process called electrolysis - the splitting - of water, that can use more power than would potentially be gained.

One of the reasons Iceland has moved ahead is that it has the benefit of large amounts of cheap, carbon-neutral renewable power (from the volcanic geothermal heat beneath the island) with which to produce hydrogen by electrolysis.

Is hydrogen expensive?

Yes. New technology, the cost of fuel cells, and the infrastructure needed to support them, far outweigh the costs of alternative fuel supplies.

Furthermore, because hydrogen holds relatively low energy per cubic metre, it would require huge containers to hold the hydrogen needed for meaningful use.

Can hydrogen ever be more than a Tomorrow's World technology?

Maybe, but fundamental research is still needed to handle the three problems - efficient and clean production of hydrogen, storage and cost.

HYDROGEN / THE ISSUES

Hydrogen technology is only at the trial stage.

The benefits are high energy output, green credentials and potential availability.

The challenges are cost, production and storage.

The Key Players

*The people and institutions that will
influence our lives in the UK*

THE KEY PLAYERS

The Key Players takes a look at the people, institutions and countries that will influence our lives.

THE DECISION MAKERS

The UK government: What is their position on our energy future?

Labour stresses the importance of maintaining a mix of energy sources, its most controversial move being the backing of a new generation of nuclear power stations.

What do the opposition parties think?

The **Tories** also back nuclear, but as a "last resort", though details of their "first resorts" are still fuzzy. **David Cameron** has put a wind turbine on his house, though. The **Liberal Democrats** are strongly anti-nuclear, seeing a future with greater "micro-generation" in homes and businesses.

Who guides the government on its decisions?

Sir David King, the government's chief scientific advisor, would have been heavily involved in the decision to back nuclear. This brought the accusation that he had "lost his bottle" from **George Monbiot**, a prominent environmental columnist for **The Guardian**.

THE INFLUENCERS

Who lobbies for the oil industry?

The UK **Offshore Operators Association** provides a focus for the companies working in British waters. This includes "The Big Five" - from the US, **Exxon Mobil** and **Chevron**, from the UK, **BP** and **Shell**, and France's **Total**. These companies also lobby individually.

And for nuclear?

The Nuclear Industry Association, representing over 100 UK-based companies, provides a central voice for the nuclear industry. Others include the private companies hoping for a stake in future plans. **British Energy**, which runs eight of the UK's nuclear power stations, plays a prominent role, but is dwarfed by European power giants such as France's **EDF** (which runs 58 stations in France) and Germany's **E:ON** and **RWE**. Future nuclear engineering is likely to be handled by either France's **Areva** or the US's **Westinghouse** and **General Electric.**

Are there other advocates of nuclear?

"Outside" the nuclear industry there is also the **Supporters of Nuclear Energy** (SONE) who are vocal in the media with **Sir Bernard Ingham**, Thatcher's former press secretary, standing as a figurehead.

Has the renewable energy industry found any "official" voices?

The British Wind Energy Association and the **Renewable Energy Association** combine the bright young things of renewable enterprise with the big companies (e.g. BP, Shell) who are also wetting their whiskers.

What about the environmentalists?

The major players are **Friends of the Earth** and **Greenpeace**. There is the government's independent watchdog on environmental matters - the **Sustainable Development Commission** chaired by **Jonathon Porritt**. Published monthly, **The Ecologist** is edited by the wealthy **Zac Goldsmith**, who has also been co-opted to develop the Conservative environmental policy.

Who educates the public on green matters?

Al Gore, who lost to **George W Bush** in the 2000 US election, has recast himself as environmental evangelist, touring the world alongside his chilling film *An Inconvenient Truth*. In the UK, the government-funded **Energy Saving Trust** and **Carbon Trust** are trying to teach homeowners and businesses how to lighten their carbon footprint.

THE MONEY MAKERS

Apart from the "Big Five", who else is making money out of oil?

The last decade has seen the rise of the supermarkets in the petrol business - **Tesco**, **Asda** and **Sainsbury's** - who now own nearly 40% of the market. Over the same period the number of independent retailers has halved.

Who is going to make money out of the new generation of nuclear power stations?

As yet, it's unclear, though likely to be the same group as the nuclear lobbyists. Of the existing power operators, **British Energy** is the least healthy, having required financial mouth-to-mouth, and, more recently, suffered operational headaches.

What about renewable energy?

Its future may fall into the hands of the bigger established companies, for example, **BP** and **Shell**, who both have active research divisions. **Scottish Power** is set to build the **Whitelee wind farm**, Europe's largest on-shore facility, on Eaglesham moor, near Glasgow. **Shell** and **E:ON** have recently been given the go-ahead to build the London Array off-shore wind farm in the Thames estuary, the biggest in the world.

What about new players in the renewable energy sector?

They could be big and small. German giant **Bosch** has entered into partnership with small companies **Lunar** and **Rotech** on a large tidal project in the Orkneys. Wave energy pilot project **Pelamis** has recently started in **Portugal**.

On a high street (or out-of-town shopping centre) near you, **B&Q** offers wind turbines and solar panels. Green energy suppliers such as **Ecotricity** and **Green Energy** are going head-to-head with the big power suppliers for the domestic market.

THE GLOBAL PLAYERS

Who are the world's leading energy consumers?
The **USA** and **China**, who are also the world's biggest carbon emitters. Neither are signed up to the **Kyoto Agreement**.

What is the USA's environmental position?
The **USA** has not backed **Kyoto** as it fears it will give countries such as **China** and **India** (who are not obliged to sign up) an unfair economic advantage. It sees voluntary emissions cuts and technological innovation as the way forward. Some fear that **George W Bush** is led by the oil lobby, including **Exxon Mobil** and **the American Petroleum Institute.**

Comparison of USA and China energy sources
Units: Percent share of world consumption

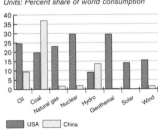

Source: BP Statistical Review 2006

At a state level, there is more activity. California, under **Governor (Arnie) Shwarzenegger**, has set up an emissions trading scheme. The mayors of over 200 major US cities have agreed to follow the aims of **Kyoto**.

What is the situation in China?
Coal will continue to power **China's** growth, though the Chinese government recognises, on paper at least, a need to curb its carbon output. Hydro-electric power on a huge scale, most notably the damming of the **Yangtsee River** at **Three Gorges Dam**, will provide the bulk of the renewables, and greater nuclear build is also likely.

Who controls the future of oil?
OPEC is main the power broker in the oil market, especially now production in the North Sea and Gulf of Mexico is in decline. **OPEC** works on a quota system, releasing a pre-agreed amount of oil so as neither to flood nor starve the market and to keep a

53

high, but stable, oil price.
The greatest proportion of the
reserves sit in **Saudi Arabia**,
who act as de facto head of
the organisation.

What about Iran and Iraq?
Iran has 10% of the world's oil
and 15% of the natural gas.
It is also embarking on a
controversial programme to
develop nuclear power
capacity, which has lead to a
stand-off with the **USA** and
the **EU**.

Iran's troubled neighbour, **Iraq**,
has the third largest oil
reserves in the world. These
are in the hands of the newly
elected Iraqi government, but
the fate of the reserves will be
intertwined with the fate of the
country as a whole.

What about Russia?
Russia has 5% of the world's
oil and 25% of the natural gas.
There is nervousness over how
President Putin will use
his influence.

*How will the European
Union impact on the
UK's decisions?*
Perhaps the biggest influence
will be through the **European
Emissions Trading Scheme**.
A fixed number of carbon
permits are made available and
companies are allowed to trade
these permits depending on
their carbon needs.
The scheme effectively puts a
price on carbon emissions.
Air traffic was previously
excluded but is now likely to
be involved.

Stargazing

What would be a good and bad scenario come 2030?

STARGAZING

So where might we end up? The Stargazing section looks at two possible scenarios – one good, one bad – for where the UK might be in 2030.

DOING WELL
A rise in renewable energy, a fall in carbon emissions, less dependency on imports.

Overall
The UK has benefited from a new spirit of international collaboration on energy technology. Carbon emissions in the UK have been falling since 2010 - and are now stabilising around the world - whilst nearly 60% of the UK's energy is "home-grown".

The rise of renewables
Wind power - both on and off shore - and a range of tidal installations along the western coast of the UK have led the surge in renewable energy generation which now supplies over a third of the UK's energy needs. Costs have fallen and a greater number of installations have improved reliability.

Successive governments have provided financial incentives for homes and businesses to micro-generate energy - mainly solar panels for electricity and water heating - as well as enforcing greater energy efficiencies in homes, offices and factories. Over 60% of all UK homes are now carbon neutral.

Carbon captured
Carbon capture and storage (CCS) is commercially proven, with the UK storing its carbon from coal fired power stations in empty oil reservoirs beneath the North Sea. Only a small amount of the UK's energy now comes from natural gas, mainly through the Norwegian Langeled pipeline and imported LNG from the Far East.

Nuclear build
Although CCS has come of age, 12 new nuclear power stations have been built, the most recent two being

"breeder" power stations, using technology first developed in India. Waste - currently shipped to Finland for burial within the earth's crust - is still a matter of controversy. As yet, all nuclear build has been privately financed, though concerns surround the costs and management of closing them down.

Oil drain

On the road, oil is still the dominant fuel, but imported bio-fuels from Eastern Europe, and new hydrogen cars from Japan, are cutting into its monopoly. Higher oil prices and toll roads - along with greater investment in the railway network - have led to a decline in road traffic. An airline fuel tax means that air traffic has not grown significantly for a decade.

Around the world

China has managed to contain its carbon releases through CCS and huge hydro-electric projects, though the latter have caused wide human and environmental disruption. The USA has become the key agent in sharing knowledge, leading to the break-through in fuel-cell technology and the Russian model for "breeder" nuclear reactors. Iran is running a peaceful, civil nuclear programme. Scientists still happy due to fusion joke.

MUST TRY HARDER
Stuttering renewables, unshackled carbon, dependency on Russia and an unstable Middle East

Overall

The world still depends on fossil fuels, with tension increasing in the Middle East as nations look to secure their supplies. In the UK, neither nuclear nor renewables are trusted to fill the energy gap. Carbon emissions continue to rise both here and across the world, with the effects of global warming becoming more consistently evident.

Unsettled nuclear

A foiled terrorist attack at a French nuclear plant in 2008 reignited public safety fears and resulted in new investment in the UK's nuclear programme

59

stalling. With only one new power station built, and the older generation expiring, nuclear now provides only a trickle of the UK's needs.

Renewables fall short

Despite some growth, mostly from wind power, renewables fell far short of the UK's "20% by 2020" target. Tidal and wave power projects are still at the pilot stage.

Prolonged political instability, partly induced by the pressure of high oil and gas prices, has led to a lack of central direction on both renewable energy policies and energy efficiency measures.

Early popularity of micro-generation technologies has tailed off after the press lambasted both their cost and efficiency.

A fossil future

CCS was returned to the drawing board, following the discovery of pollution in North Sea fish. Imported coal is still an important fuel in the UK, but is also a major polluter. Many power companies have dropped co-firing with biomass due to the cost.

With Norwegian reserves now drained, the UK has become more reliant on an increasingly powerful Russia for natural gas. Shortages in the unexpected cold snap winters of 2020 and 2021 led to widespread power-cuts, the like of which were last seen in the 1970's.

Oil slick

The price of oil continues to hover around $100 a barrel (it ended 2006 at $60). In the UK, hybrid cars are more common than petrol and diesel models, though the new Japanese hydrogen cars were a flop due to a tendency to explode.

Air traffic has continued to increase. A new runway has been built at Heathrow with two others due to open at Manchester and Stansted. Airlines have committed to offset carbon emissions, though the transparency of these schemes has been attacked by environmentalists.

Dirty world

The failure of "big" clean coal technologies means that China has overtaken the USA as the world's great polluter. Tension continues to escalate in the Middle East over the remaining oil supplies, though reserves from the Canadian oil sands have gone a little way to dissipate this. Large-scale droughts in both Africa and Bangladesh are commonplace and there is increased flooding in major cities such as London and Shanghai.

What can you do?

How you can make a mark

WHAT CAN YOU DO?

The big issues – energy security, global warming, the energy gap – are not easy to grasp, let alone influence. But can you do anything to really make a difference?

Cut the waste

Energy efficiency is the buzz phrase. Tips range from the simple, cost-free - turn off lights, close the curtains, turn down thermostat, don't leave the TV on stand-by - to the more complicated and not-free - energy-saving lightbulbs, cavity wall and loft insulation, double-glazing.

You can find out more by visiting Energy Saving Trust, **www.est.org.uk,** the Carbon Trust, **www.carbontrust.co.uk.**

First Step

Commit to save 20% of your energy with the Energy Saving Trust. Visit www.est.org.uk/commit.

Buy green

The Renewables Obligation means that all the big power companies will have to offer more and more renewable energy over the next decade. You can also switch to a green supplier, for example Green Energy, **www.greenenergy.uk.com**, that promises to source from, and invest in, renewable energies. There has been some criticism of power companies not being entirely clear on what their "green" tariffs include.

First Step

Compare the tariffs of energy suppliers at the Green Electricity Marketplace, www.greenelectricity.org.

Do-it-yourself

Now it gets more glamorous. Solar panels and wind turbines are now available on the High Street - look at B&Q, **www.diy.com**

Not all houses are suitable. Wind turbines need clear access to the prevalent wind, whilst solar panels require south facing walls.

The costs of a wind turbine start from around £1,500 and for solar water heating about £2,000, depending on the number of panels you need.

Planning permission is needed so check with the local authority before installing. It is estimated, though not proven, that you will get "payback" on investment in 5 and 10 years.
First Step
Look at available grants and accredited installers at Low Carbon Buildings, www.lowcarbonbuildings. org.uk.

Micro-generate some cash
You'll hear a lot about selling excess energy back to the national grid. But how does this work, and can you make money?

If you wire your solar panel or wind turbine into the grid then you can sell surplus energy back to your power company, who are obliged to pay you for this. A drawback is that they purchase at 2-3p per kWh rather than the 10-12p they sell it at. In Germany, where micro-generation is vastly more popular, the power companies have to pay five times more.

To monitor your energy production you could fit an "export meter" (expensive) or you could cut a deal with a renewables power company - for example Good Energy, **www.good-energy.co.uk** - and they will pay you a higher rate of 4p per kWh depending on the type of generation.
First Step
Call your power company to see what they currently offer.

Car works
Emissions from road traffic make up nearly 30% of the UK's total (though one long-haul flight equates to a year's worth of driving). Most of us need cars, but what, apart from squeezing on a cycling helmet, can we do to lessen our impact?

You could use one of the greener fuels available. Blended bio-fuel is available at many garages, including Tesco and BP. The majority of current engines can be converted to accept LPG (a less polluting and lower taxed fuel) and still run on petrol. Visit Greenfuel, **www.greenfuel.org.uk,** for an online quote. Prices start from £500.

When in the market for a new car, look for cars that run on less carbon-emitting fuels, LPG or diesel. You could consider a hybrid or battery-run car.
First Step
Look for a blended biofuel when you next fill up your tank.

Come back down to earth
Carbon emissions from flying now stand at 6% of the UK total. If air travel grows as predicted this could rise as high as 50% by 2030. Greenhouse gases emitted by planes have nearly three times the warming effect of those released at ground level. Flying less is one option, as is carbon offsetting (see below).
First Step
If you want to fly less, especially short-haul, check out the pan-European train timetable from the German rail company, Deutsche Bahn. http://reiseauskunft.bahn.de.

Offset your carbon emissions
You can negate your carbon emissions by paying a fee to a company who will invest in a carbon reducing scheme,

usually tree planting or a renewable energy project.

The amount you pay is based on what you wish to offset – from a single plane journey to your year's carbon emissions (energy consumption, car and plane journeys).

Environmentalists have concerns about carbon offsetting, concerned that the schemes do not provide a true "offset" and that it removes our personal responsibility to make a lasting difference.

The UK's government plans to introduce a new "Gold Standard" for offsetters. Currently the companies who comply are Pure, **www.puretrust.org.uk**, Global Cool, **www.global-cool.com**, Equiclimate, **www.ebico.co.uk**, and Carbon Offsets, **www.carbon-offsets.com.**
First Step
Compare the services of the four "Gold Standard" companies.

Take a stand

Can you do anything to influence the big questions? Cast your vote carefully, based on each party's energy policies. Write a letter to your MP. Then write another one.

Join a pressure group – there are many to choose from. If you are pro-renewable (and anti-nuclear) you may have more choice. Greenpeace, **www.greenpeace.org.uk,** or Friends of the Earth, **www.foe.co.uk,** are obvious starters. If you are pro-nuclear, take a look at Supporters of Nuclear Energy, **www.sone.org.uk.**
First Step
Write to your MP, a directory of contacts is available at www.parliament.org.

Further Reading

The best places to keep up-to-date

FURTHER READING

A full list of the sources used in this Pocket Issue guide and other further reading is available on the website, **www.pocket*issue*.com.**

Hopefully this Pocket Issue has given you some confidence to stump up an opinion from the dinner table to water cooler. You should now be able to make out those of your family, friends and colleagues who speak sense, and those who, well, don't. Here's our quick guide to going deeper and finding out more about the issues.

Government Policy
Visit the Department of Trade and Industry website to read a copy of the government's Energy Review and ongoing policy amendments.
www.dti.gov.uk

The Stern Report - the report on the economics of climate change - is available on the Treasury's website.
www.hm-treasury.gov.uk

Technology
There are a number of sites on the oil industry (many self-interested) so a good starting place for research is the online encyclopedia, Wikipedia.
www.wikipedia.org

The technology for natural gas is well covered by the Natural Gas Institute, www.naturalgas.org, likewise coal on the World Coal Institute.
www.worldcoal.org

Find out more on nuclear technology on the World Nuclear Association.
www.world-nuclear.org

A good Q&A briefing on wind, wave and tidal power is available on the British Wind Energy Assocation.
www.bwea.com

There is lots of information on the micro-generation technologies on the Low Carbon Buildings website.
www.lowcarbonbuildings.org.uk

Climate Change

The Met Office's Hadley Centre is one of the leading research centres in the world for the science and potential effects of climate change.
www.metoffice.gov.uk

Statistics

There is good statistical information on the world's energy habits on the International Energy Agency website,
www.iea.org, the US government site,
www.eia.doe.gov,
and the oil company BP,
www.bp.com.

Keep up to date with developments on the Pocket Issue website,
www.pocket*issue*.com.
Other good sources are the BBC,
www.bbc.co.uk,
and The Guardian,
www.guardian.co.uk.

The Glossary

Jargon-free explanations

THE GLOSSARY

A glossary of words, some scientific, some strange, some ugly that have appeared in this book, and you will probably hear in the media.

Auto-gas
The same as Liquified Petroleum Gas.

Biomass or bio-fuel
Fuel made from plant or animal origins - e.g. ethanol distilled from sugar cane to power cars, natural gas from rotting landfill sites.

Breeder Reactor
A nuclear reactor deliberately designed to create fuel as its consumes it. Pros: Breeder reactors use the more common Uranium-238, producing less waste. Cons: Uneconomic. There is only one nuclear power station using breeder technology in the world today, in Russia.

Carbon Capture and Storage (CCS)
Capturing and storing carbon dioxide (CO2) released by power stations before it reaches the atmosphere. Pros: Allows fossil fuels to be burned in less environmental damaging way. Cons: Unproven and uncertain impact on environment.

Carbon Dioxide, CO2
Gas released when fossil fuels are burned and the most important greenhouse gas behind water vapour.

Carbon Neutral
An activity or journey which doesn't create carbon dioxide.

Carbon off setting
Indidviduals or companies investing in green schemes - e.g. tree planting - to counter the carbon generated in their day-to-day lives. Environmentalists have serious doubts, with concerns over their true effectiveness and that offsetting allows people to avoid changing their behaviour.

Carbon Sequestration
A fancy word for carbon capture and storage.

Carbon Tax
A tax on carbon dioxide emissions.

Carbon Trading
Sometimes called Cap and Trade. A means to reduce carbon emissions. Governments issue a fixed number of carbon credits, and allow institutions to buy or sell these credits depending on their carbon needs. Effectively puts a price on carbon emissions. The biggest scheme in the world is the EU's Emissions Trading Scheme (ETS).

Chain Reaction
The process by which heat is created in nuclear fission. An atom is split and releases energy and neutrons. The neutrons then split more atoms, each time releasing more energy and neutrons. And so forth.

Chernobyl
Accident at Ukrainian nuclear power station in 1986. Left 30 dead, many more with cancer and dispersed radioactive contamination across a vast area of Europe.

CHP, Combined Heat & Power
A power station, often small-scale, that allows its waste heat to be used by neighbouring facitilies.

Clean Development Mechanism (CDM)
An agreement at the Kyoto meeting of 1997 that developed countries could invest in carbon-reducing schemes in the developing world as part of their commitment to reduce their own emissions.

Climate Change
Climate change is the warming or cooling of the Earth, and how this affects the climates of local areas over the short and long-term, for example greater rainfall or changing average temperatures

Co-Firing
Burning biomass with coal in power stations to reduce carbon emissions.

Crude Oil
Raw oil, before it has been refined into end products such as petrol, diesel or kerosene.

Distributed Energy
Small to medium-scale energy generation that primarily feeds local communities rather than the national grid.

Electricity
A form of energy created from primary fuels such as coal or natural gas. Generated by copper wires picking up an electrical charge when being passed through magnetic fields.

Electrolysis
Splitting water to get hold of hydrogen. Currently uses more energy than the hydrogen would produce.

Energy Efficiency
Saving energy rather than using it. It is cheaper to save one KW of energy than to produce it.

Energy Gap
The difference between the energy we need and the energy we can produce. A specific problem for the UK due to the scheduled closure of old nuclear and coal-fired power stations.

Energy Security
The control a nation has over its own

energy supplies. The more energy it imports, generally the less secure it is.

Enriched Uranium
Uranium usually contains 1% of the isotope U-235. Enriched uranium for use in nuclear power stations contains 2-3% of U-235. Enrichment is by chemical diffusion or mechanical spinning.

Ethanol
Alcohol fermented from sugar cane and used as a fuel for transport. Over 90% is produced in the USA and Brazil.

European Emissions Trading Scheme
A pan-EU carbon trading scheme, the biggest in the world.

Fission
The process of splitting an atom to release energy. Currently, all nuclear power stations in the world use nuclear fission.

Fossil Fuels
General name given to oil, natural gas and coal.

Fuel Cell
A chemical "battery" that needs no recharging or changing as long as it has access to fuel.

Fusion
The joining of an atom to release energy. Pros: Less harmful waste, no need for chain reaction, plenty of reserves of fuel. Cons: Fusion is commercially unproven, drawing more energy than it creates.

Gas Hydrates
Methane and frozen water, found deep on the ocean floor. At the moment not economic to drill for but may be released by global warming.

Gasification
Another means of carbon capture. Creating a gas of carbon monoxide and hydrogen from fossil fuels and capturing the excess carbon.

Global Warming
Increases in the average temperature in the world.

Greenhouse Gases
Gases in the atmosphere - the main being water vapour, carbon dioxide and methane - that maintain warmth on our planet. Man-made increases of greenhouse gases, predominently carbon dioxide and methane, are suspected of causing global warming.

Ground Source Heat Pumps
Renewable energy technology that draws heat from the soil.

Hiroshima
Atomic bomb dropped by the Allied Forces on Japanese city of Hiroshima in August 1945, killing an estimated 140,000 people.

Hybrid cars
Cars that are fuelled by a combination of petrol and electric battery.

Hydrogen
The most common element in the universe, and a potential source of energy when burned as a gas or charging a fuel cell. Pros: Clean, efficient and global availability. Cons: Difficult to produce economically, cost of technology, and storage.

Hydro (electric) Power
Power created by the movement of water. Usually generated by damming rivers and controlling the flow of water to turn turbines. Currently the biggest source of renewable energy in the world. Pros: Carbon free power. Cons: Environmental damage, best sites often exploited so limited future growth.

Isotopes
Atoms of the same element but with different atomic weight, based on the number of neutrons in the atom.

Kerosene
A refined oil, the main aviation fuel.

kW (Kilowatt)
A thousand watts.

kWh (Kilowatt hour)
The unit of power consumption or generation. The number of Kilowatts used or made in an hour. The average consumption of a UK household is around 4000 kWh each year.

Kyoto Agreement
1997 UN agreement between developed countries to cut their greenhouse emissions by, on average, 5% below 1990 levels. The UK aims for 12%. The USA and Australia have not signed up. China and India are not obliged to participate.

Langeled
Pipeline carrying natural gas from Norway to the UK. Opened in 2006.

LNG, Liquified Natural Gas.
Natural gas compressed into a liquid. Pros: Increases diversity of world supply, less reliance on pipelines. Cons: Costly and explosive.

Load factor
A measurement of the actual electricity generation against theoretical total capacity. Renewable energy sources have a lower load factor compared to fossil fuels and nuclear.

London Array
Potentially the world's biggest off-shore wind farm, to be built in the Thames Estuary by a consortium that include Shell and E:ON. Has recently been given the go-ahead by the government.

LPG, Liquid Petroleum Gas

Gases - propane, butane, or a mixture of both - that can be pressurised and turned into liquids. A natural by-product of drilling for oil or can be refined from crude. A greener and less taxed fuel.

Methane

The main component of natural gas. Also a greenhouse gas, with seven times the heat-trapping capacity of carbon dioxide (but a much shorter lifespan in the atmosphere).

Micro-generation

Small scale energy production, usually below 50KW. Often refers to generation at homes and offices. Examples include solar panels for electricity or water heating or "mini" wind-turbines.

National Grid

The network that moves electricity from power stations to homes, offices and factories.

Nuclear Energy

Energy created from either splitting (nuclear fission) or joining (nuclear fusion) atoms.

Nuclear Reactor

An installation that creates nuclear energy.

Nuclear waste

The waste products from nuclear power stations. Usually referring to the waste that is radioactive, such as the spent fuel.

On-shore wind energy

Wind turbines situated on land. Most current wind energy in the UK is created on-shore

Oil sands

Deposits of bitumen, a viscous oil that will not flow unless heated or mixed with lighter oils. Main reserves found in Canada and Venezuala. Pros: An alternative source of oil. Cons: Expensive to produce and more carbon than regular oil.

OPEC,

The Organisation of Petroleum Exporting Countries. A group of countries that aims to maintain a good, stable price for oil in the world's markets, without diverting customers to alternative energy sources. Members are Saudi Arabia, Iran, Iraq, UAE, Kuwait, Qatar, Algeria, Nigeria, Libya, Indonesia and Venezuala.

Passively Safe

Technology that closes down a nuclear power station without the need for human intervention.

Peak Oil Theory

The date that world oil production peaks and subsequently begins its decline - the date we start running out of oil. Estimates range from 2008 to 2040.

Photovoltaic

Solar panels that create electricity directly from sunlight as opposed to heating water.

Radioactive waste

The waste from nuclear power stations that is radioactive and extremely harmful to living things. Takes hundreds or thousands of years to become safe.

Renewable Energy

Energy from sources that are not going to deplete within a human timespan, hundreds or thousands of years. Examples include solar power, wind power, and wave and tidal power.

Renewables Obligation

Government legislation requiring UK power companies to source 15% of their power from renewable energy sources. This is likely to rise to 20% in any new government energy bill.

Reprocessing

Working through nuclear waste to find elements that can be reused as nuclear fuel. Pros: Recycling, reducing radioactivity of waste. Cons: Costly, bad environmental record, concerns over nuclear elements falling into wrong hands.

Reserves

The amount of an energy source that is economically realistic to recover. Estimates look at proven, probable and possible reserves.

Sell-Back

The ability of small-scale energy producers (micro-generation or distributed energy) to sell back any excess energy generated to the national grid.

Solar Panels

Panels that use the heat of the sun to create energy - either electrical through photovoltaic, or by heating water.

Spinning Reserve

The amount of back-up energy kept in reserve to cover any potential short-falls in an installation's electricity production.

Stern Report

Government commissioned report, published in 2006 by Sir Nicholas Stern, that examined the economics of climate change.

Tidal energy
Energy generated by the flow of water drawn back and forth by tides. Still in pilot stage.

Thorium
A naturally occuring element that could be used in nuclear fission. It creates the fissionable isotope Uranium-233. India, which has 25% of the world's thorium is designing its nuclear reactors to use it.

Turbine
Device that turns the magnets in the creation of electricity in power stations.

Uranium
A naturally occurring mineral in the world and a major fuel for nuclear power stations. Biggest reserves in Australia, Canada and Kazakhstan.

Uranium-235
An isotope of uranium that is prone to fission. The main fuel for nuclear power stations. Uranium contains only 1% U-235. Needs to be enriched to 2-3% for use.

Uranium-238
An isotope of uranium. U-238 makes up 99% of the world's uranium. Can be used in breeder reactors, being turned into the fissionable Plutonium-239.

Volt
Unit of electrical potential - like the water pressure in a hose pipe.

Watt
Unit of power generation.

Wave energy
Energy generated by harnessing the movement of the waves. Still in pilot stage. Storm waves in the Atlantic and North Sea could be productive in the future

Whitelee
Europe's largest on-shore wind farm, to be built by Scottish Power close to Glasgow.

Wind Turbine
Turbine that harnesses the wind to generate electricity. Can be in large-scale "farms" or micro-generating "mini" versions on homes and offices. Wind power currently creates less than 1% of UK's energy, but is a big hope for the future.